mother & daughter

robbin rawlings

Contents

Contents

The Best Part of us...

Photo of me

Photo of you

...is When We are Together

Photo of you & me!

Anywhere we go
People can see
How happy we are
To be with one another

This is Where We come From

You were born... 12-2015

Some special things about where you were born...

I was born...

Some special things about where I was born...

My first recollection of you...

_____

_____

_____

_____

_____

_____

Your first recollection of me...

_____

_____

_____

_____

_____

In the same instant,
One becomes mother
One becomes daughter

our childhoods

Your favorite childhood memory...

_____
_____
_____
_____
_____

My favorite childhood memory...

_____
_____
_____
_____
_____
_____

Those things we both did as little girls...

_____

_____

_____

_____

_____

You were surprised when I...

_____

_____

_____

_____

the tree
and the sapling

Photo

Our Best Times

Some of your favorite memories of the early days with me...

_____

_____

_____

_____

_____

_____

Some of my favorite memories of the early days with you...

_____

_____

_____

_____

Now, as adults, your favorite memories of us...

_____

_____

_____

_____

_____

And my favorite memories of us as adults...

_____

_____

Something you did that made me so happy...

_____

_____

Something I did that made you extremely happy...

_____

_____

what more pure
to love the child
born of your womb

Our Worst Times

The more trying times in the early days were...

_____

_____

_____

_____

_____

The more difficult times in recent years were...

_____

_____

_____

_____

_____

_____

How living through those times made our bond stronger...

_____

_____

_____

_____

_____

What I learned from you then...

_____

_____

_____

_____

_____

What you learned from me then...

_____

_____

_____

_____

in your shadow I lay
when the heat is too much
yet it's your warmth
that keeps me alive

Our Family

These are some of the important members of our family...

Photo

Photo

The greatest influences
Come from close by...

Your favorite family events...
_____
_____
_____

My favorite family events...
_____
_____

Traditions that we've had through the years...:
_____
_____
_____
_____
_____

Others We Consider Family

Photo

Photo

Photo

Photo

Those special things we always do when we are all together...

_____

_____

_____

_____

_____

_____

The best family reunion we've had so far...

_____

_____

_____

The oddest family reunion was...

_____

_____

_____

love reflects
off of our faces...

Our Favorite Spring Moments

These are the special things we like to do during the spring months...

_____

_____

_____

_____

_____

_____

_____

_____

Special days we celebrate during spring...

_____

_____

_____

_____

_____

Our best springtime memory is...

_____

_____

_____

_____

_____

_____

_____

_____

_____

_____

Photo

Photo

Our Birthdays

Your birthday is
_____

Different ways we've made it special through the years...
_____

_____

_____

_____

Some special things about your birth and youth...
_____

_____

_____

What you think of most on your birthday...
_____

_____

_____

My birthday is

Different ways we've made it special through the years...

Some special things about my birth and youth...

What I think of most on my birthday...

Other Special Days

Some of your special days we celebrate and the things we do then...

_____

_____

_____

Some of my special days we celebrate and the things we do then...

_____

_____

_____

Some special people you also like to celebrate with...

_____

_____

_____

Some special people I also like to celebrate with...

_____

_____

_____

The most special day of the year for us is...

_____

_____

_____

and this is what we do then...

_____

_____

_____

_____

A memorable one was when...

_____

_____

_____

_____

no matter
what destiny
brings us
our bond is forever

How We are the Same

There are some special things that we have in common. These are just a few...

_____

_____

_____

_____

_____

Because of you, these things have changed in me...

_____

_____

Because you are such a role model, I have changed in these ways...

_____

_____

the beauty
of mothers and daughters
is in the looks they share
in the touch they bestow
to one another

How We are Different

There are some special things that make us different. These are just a few...

_____
_____
_____
_____
_____
_____

Some things not even you could make me like...

_____
_____
_____

Some things not even I could make you like...

_____
_____
_____
_____

tell me how I can grow
to be half as wonderful

as you

Admiration, Admiration

Things I admire in you...

Things you admire in me...

Things I know about you and your character that still astonish me and fill me with pride...

_____
_____
_____
_____
_____
_____

Things you've seen in me that you admire...

_____
_____

a
mutual
admiration
society
mother & daughter

Our Trips Together

The first trip I remember with you...

_____

_____

_____

The first time you took me on a trip was...

_____

_____

_____

What was special about that trip...

_____

_____

_____

Remember when we went away, just you and I? We went to...

_____

_____

_____

Some special things we did on that trip that we decided we should do again...

_____

_____

_____

What I like most about travelling with you...

_____

_____

_____

What you like most about travelling with me...

_____

_____

_____

Few are the things I'd rather do
than spend time with you...

Our Favorite Summer Moments

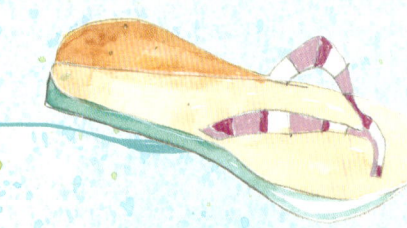

These are the special things we like to do during the summer months...

_____

_____

_____

_____

_____

_____

Special days we celebrate during summer...

_____

_____

_____

_____

_____

Our favorite summer memory is...

_____

_____

_____

_____

_____

_____

_____

_____

Photo

mothers are the trees
under which daughters
look for shade and shelter...

Photo

Photo

Those Wondrous Things
We See in Each Other

I feel the most special traits you have are...

_____

_____

_____

_____

What you would consider to be my best traits...

_____

_____

_____

Some traits we share...

_____

_____

_____

Like bells,
no matter the tone
they always sound good
together

Our Laughs

There are some unique things you say that make me laugh...

_____

_____

_____

Those things I say that make you giggle...

_____

_____

Your favorite funny story about me...

_____

_____

_____

My favorite funny story about you...

_____

_____

_____

_____

Things We Love to Do Together

When we're together, people can tell we're glad to be together. We've heard them say...

_____

_____

_____

When we're together, everything is special because...

_____

_____

_____

Because it has such great memories for us, our favorite place to go is...

_____

_____

_____

two peas in a pod
come to mind...

Things We Do on Our Own

Togetherness is great, yet there are a few things we'd rather do alone...

_____

_____

_____

_____

There are a few things you like to do that I'm not too keen on...

_____

_____

_____

There are a few things I like to do that you're not thrilled with...

_____

_____

_____

Our Favorite Fall Moments

These are the special things we like to do during the fall months...

Special days we celebrate during fall...

Fall is a time of change and growth. Our best fall memory is...

Photo

mothers serve as guides
daughters are their reward

Photo

Photo

The Great Triumphs We've Shared

Of all the wonderful things that have happened to me, the ones I was the most excited to be able share with you were...

_____
_____
_____
_____

How we celebrated those extraordinary times...

_____
_____
_____
_____

The most wonderful things that happened to you which I was blessed to share with you...

_____
_____
_____
_____

Those Proud Moments

There have been many proud moments for both of us. Some of my favorites are...

_____

_____

_____

Some of your favorites are...

_____

_____

_____

So many things are special, but I am most proud of you because...

_____

_____

You are most proud of me because...

_____

_____

pick her out of the crowd
she will be brimming
with love and pride

The Not-So-Great Moments We've Shared

We've been through so much, you and I. Some not-so-great situations we've lived through...

_____

_____

_____

_____

One that is very funny (now that it's history) is...

_____

_____

_____

We've been there for each other through the years. Some of the sad times were...

_____

_____

_____

What I admired most about how you dealt with a situation and what I learned from it was...

_____

_____

_____

_____

The best advice you ever gave me in times of trouble...

_____

_____

_____

What you discovered from me during times of trouble...

_____

_____

_____

How we helped each other cope...

_____

_____

_____

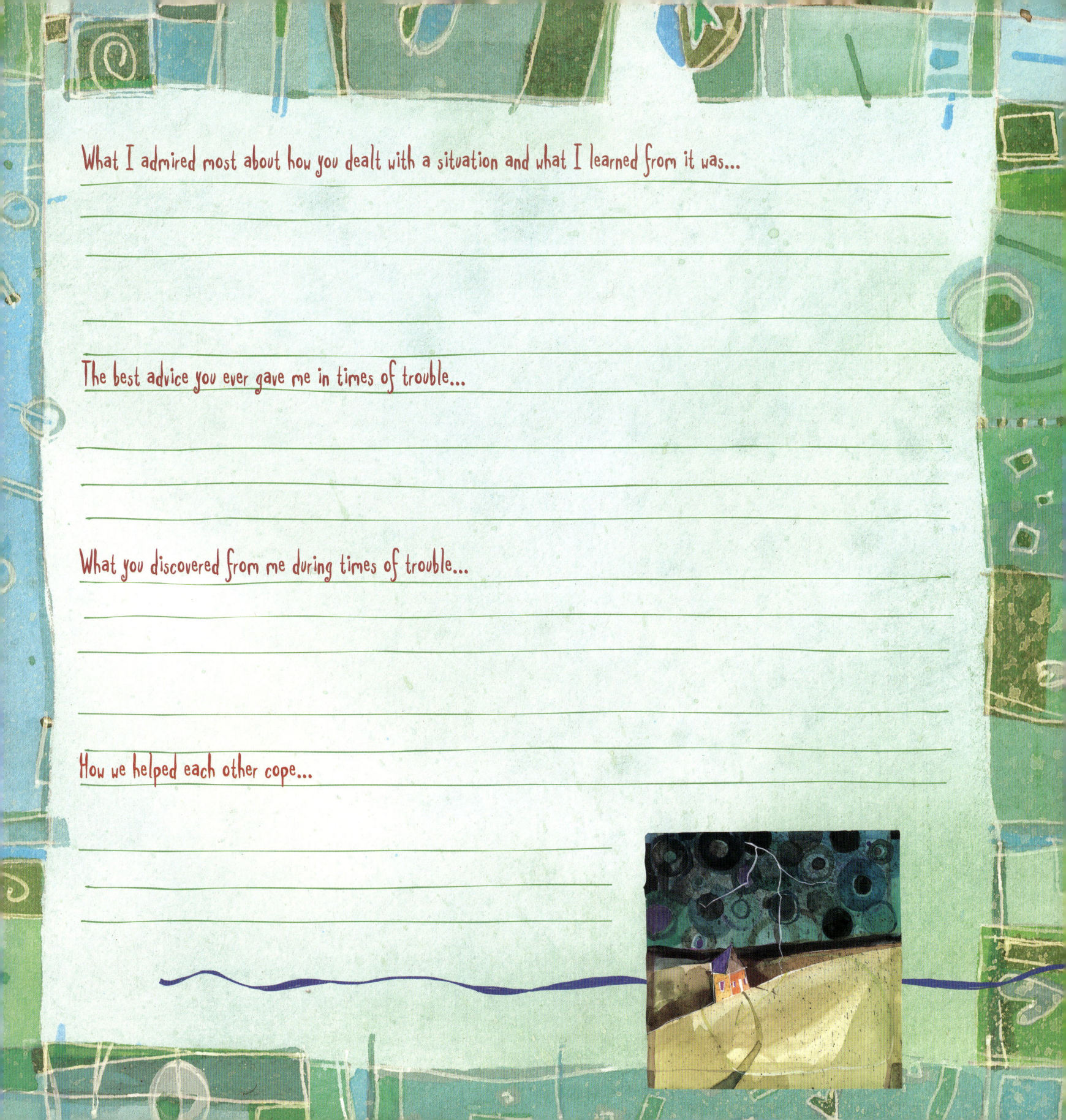

Then There's Food

What you like best to eat...

_____

_____

_____

Preparation is part of the enjoyment. What you love to make for me is...

_____

_____

_____

What I enjoy most is...

_____

_____

_____

What I know you love and make for you...

_____

_____

_____

you never turn away...

Some foods I don't like, but I eat because of you...

_____

_____

_____

Some foods you'd never tried that I introduced to you...

_____

_____

_____

When I need comfort food, I reach for...

_____

_____

_____

Your preferred comfort food is...

_____

_____

_____

_____

Our Favorite Winter Moments

These are the special things we like to do during the winter months...

_____

_____

_____

_____

_____

Special days we celebrate during winter...

_____

_____

_____

_____

Photo

though the night
may be long and cold
your face gives me
peace and assurance

Winter is a time for reflection and introspection. Our favorite winter memory is...

_____

_____

_____

_____

_____

_____

_____

_____

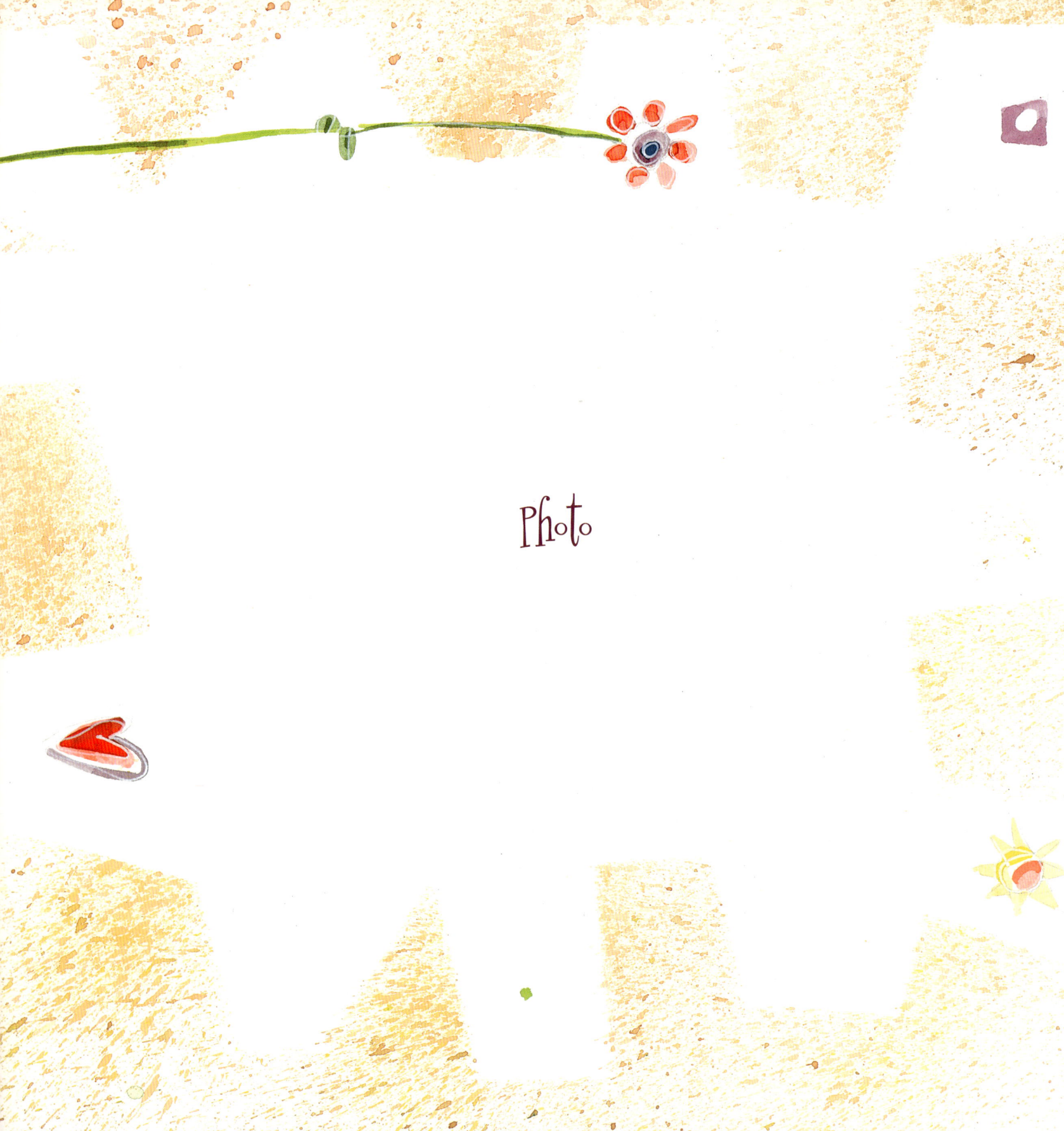

Photo

Photo

When We Go out

We have had wonderful times together. Our favorite things to do when we go out are...

Where you enjoy eating...

Where I like to go to eat...

Some of the best times we spend together are at...

one teaches how to stand

one teaches how to dance

When We Stay at Home

It can be just quiet time, or full of activity. Some of our favorite things to do at home are...

What we munch on when we're at home...

Special things we use for special occasions...

Words are Not Always easy to come by

I know you know, but I've always wanted to tell you that...

_____

_____

_____

_____

_____

_____

_____

_____

_____

You know I know, but you've always wanted to tell me that...

_____

_____

_____

_____

_____

_____

_____

_____

Just think,
once we were joined together.
Hasn't changed much, eh?

And Now, Our Future

What I would like the future to bring for you and for me...

_____

_____

_____

_____

_____

_____

_____

_____

_____

daughters give more honor
more love,
once they become mothers
themselves

What you would like the future to bring for you and for me...

_____

_____

_____

_____

_____

_____

_____

_____

giver of birth
giver of life
giver of givers